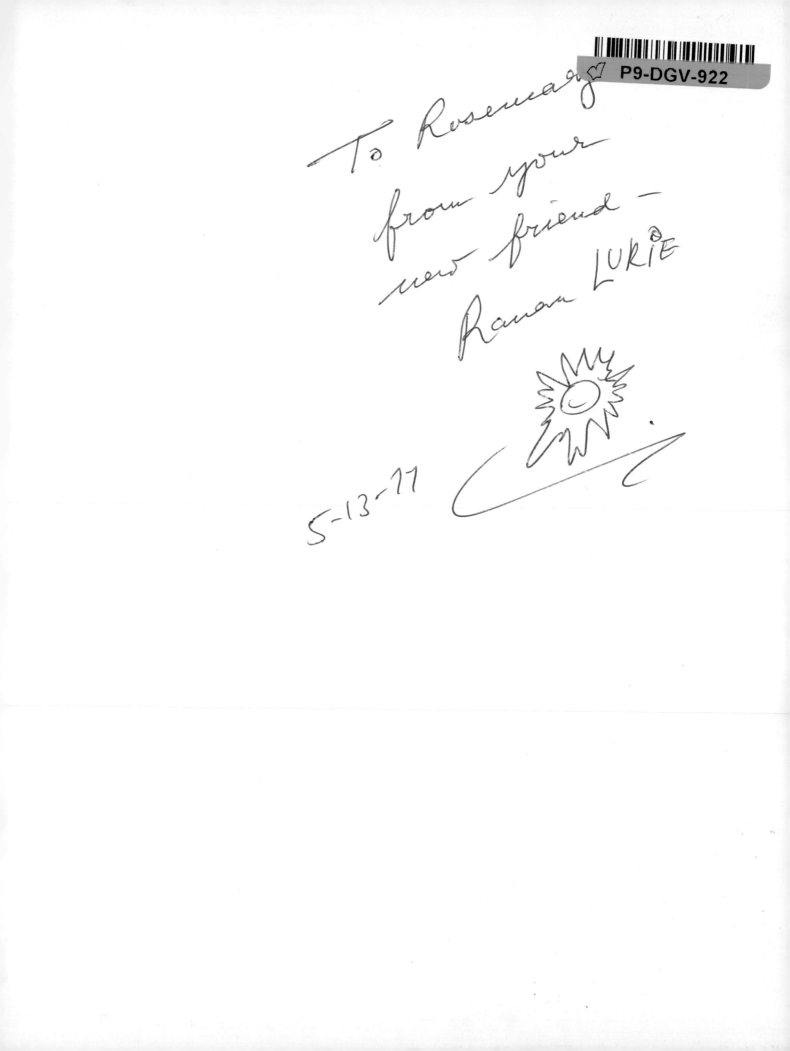

To Rosemary
from your
new friend —
Ranan LURIE

5-13-77

NI(X)ON RATED
CARTOONS

NI(X)ON RATED CARTOONS

Ranan R. Lurie

Foreword by THOMAS GRIFFITH

 Quadrangle/The New York Times Book Co.

LIBRARY OF CONGRESS CATALOG CARD NUMBER: 43-85746

INTERNATIONAL STANDARD BOOK NUMBER: 0-8129-0404-4

PRODUCTION BY PLANNED PRODUCTION

CONTENTS

THE WHITE HOUSE

WASHINGTON

March 28, 1973

Dear Mr. Lurie:

The President continues to enjoy your cartoons and expressed a
desire to add another Lurie original with your inscription to his
continually growing collection.

If the original of the enclosed cartoon commenting on the return
of the POW's from Southeast Asia which appeared on February
16th is still available, I would appreciate your sending it to me so
that I can pass it along to the President.

Many thanks and best wishes,

Sincerely,

Herbert G. Klein
Director of Communications
for the Executive Branch

Ranan R. Lurie
Baldwin Farms North
Greenwich, Connecticut 06830

April 19, 1973

Mr. Herbert G. Klein
The White House
Washington, D.C.

Dear Mr. Klein:

As usual, it is a pleasure hearing from you.

I just returned yesterday from my Australian trip, and I am
sending you today a print of the cartoon that you requested
for the President. Through our previous correspondence I have
explained that I have to keep the originals, and I appreciate
the President's generosity in understanding my approach.

Please pass to the President indirect regards from Mr. Gough
Whitlam, the new Australian Prime Minister, and several of
his Cabinet Ministers whom I had the opportunity of meeting,
talking with, and drawing. I found the new Australian men-
tality most intriguing--especially the angle they are adopting
toward the U.S.

Sincerely,

Ranan Lurie

THE WHITE HOUSE

WASHINGTON

May 9, 1973

PERSONAL

Dear Mr. Lurie:

You were most thoughtful to send me the
inscribed copy of "Reborn." Now, my
special collection can boast of yet another
Lurie cartoon! Herb Klein told me about
your recent trip to Australia, and I was
pleased to learn about the goodwill you
encountered there.

With best wishes,

Sincerely,

Richard Nixon

Mr. Ranan R. Lurie
Baldwin Farms, North
Greenwich, Connecticut 06830

FOREWORD

by Thomas Griffith,
Editor of *Life*

I first heard of Ranan Lurie back in 1967 when he wrote for *Life* magazine his tale of taking a long journey to a short war. He was the political cartoonist for the leading Israeli press, and had just opened a one-man portrait show at Expo '67 when the Middle East crisis worsened. Off he flew 6,000 miles to his homeland, led his company into battle in Jordan as an Israeli army major, acquitted himself well, and was back in Montreal within three weeks.

Ranan Lurie often goes to such great lengths to do what he believes worth doing. Shortly after the Six Day War, he began drawing editorial cartoons for *Life*, having been discovered by Bernard Quint, then *Life*'s art director. Each week *Life* would fly Lurie down from Canada, he would check in at the Waldorf-Astoria, talk over editorial ideas with us, draw them quickly, then fly back to his family in Montreal. With his soldier's lean toughness, he never seemed exhausted by the commuting, and never at a loss for ideas. His astonishing fecundity in ideas, more than his drawing, was what I first came to admire about him. As the editor of *Life*, I would show him a draft of an editorial; he would read it carefully, seize its point, ask a question or two, excuse himself and return fifteen minutes later with three or four cartoon ideas to choose from. At first, he was more at home in foreign policy than in American politics, and sometimes a subtlety of our scene had to be explained to him; but he is an amazingly quick study, and in fifteen minutes he would return again with another two or three ideas that took the troublesome nuance into account. These were all swift pencil sketches, like a child's drawings. In the beginning these same simplistic drawings, finished off in black and white ink, were what appeared in *Life*. Most European cartoonists work this way, and Lurie was in their tradition. Just as Picasso's harshest distortions gave no evidence that in other moods he could be so meticulous and sure a draftsman, I then had no idea that Lurie's artfully crude drawings concealed a gift for caricature. Gradually, with our encouragement, he began working likenesses into his drawings and they began to evolve into the Lurie style of today—large recognizable heads thrusting out of small bodies with mincing feet. You don't have to print little tags on his figures, labeling this one Laird, that one Agnew. The editor-in-chief used to complain that Lurie gave Nixon too much nose, but just as Harold Wilson and Harold Macmillan in time came to look to me like Vicky's Wilson and Macmillan, so for me the real Nixon looks more and more like Lurie's Nixon.

Lurie liked his relationship with *Life* and the visibility it gave him, but felt cramped by our insistence that his cartoon should always accompany an editorial on the subject, and in attitude not stray too far from it. Rarely did we have disputes over editorial stands. If he was troubled by the draft of an editorial, his response usually took the form of wishing its point sharpened, and if he with all his abundant repertory of metaphors had trouble finding a way to illustrate it, it behooved us to consider again whether the editorial's language was too muzzy. I enjoyed these exchanges. His manner is first to apologize for what he is about to say, but then to say something pointed and forthright; Lurie is tactful but terribly direct. Soon our sessions turned into weekly exchanges of opinion about the news, about which he had decided views. His Israeli origins make him sophisticated about military strategy, skeptical of the Communist powers, morally concerned, and personally on the side of the self-reliant.

I sympathized with his restlessness. Though Lurie insists that it is possible to draw a cartoon on any subject, we put this conviction to severe test by our insistence on writing editorials with such deadly themes as balance-of-trade payments. It was the *illustrating* part that Lurie really objected to. In this he was like a gifted accompanist who can only feel fulfilled in himself when he becomes a concert soloist. When contract renewal time came, we both compromised: In his work for us, on the editorial page or in illustrating Hugh Sidney's Washington column, his cartoons still had to bear on our subject matter, but we would no longer require exclusive rights to his work. He was free to draw cartoons for newspapers, and in a short time he built up an impressive number of clients, so that when *Life* folded in 1972, he was well established on his own. To the end though, he stayed faithful to his *Life* connection, subjecting himself to "illustrating" (as he would call it with some disdain) in a way that he would tolerate nowhere else. All this deserves telling because it is already past history for Lurie. His newspaper contracts give him undisputed editorial control; his cartoons need no one's prior approval and go out to editors untouched, with even an occasional eccentricity of spelling left uncorrected. Such unique freedom is an audacious but earned position for one who, as I write this, has lived in the United States only five years.

Lurie regards himself as a thinker who happens to draw. I'm not sure that the parallel he draws between himself and an editorial writer is as valid as he thinks It Is, nor sure that his is the kind of temperament that marshals step-by-step argumentation; but then, what editorial writer can draw? For Lurie, nonetheless, the serious business is first getting his thinking straight; once he has done that, the leap to visual metaphors and the execution are quickly done. How well he has reacted to events, at the timely moment when his response had to be swiftly decided, is evident in this book.

I used to think of Lurie as inevitably handicapped by not having spent his early life on the American scene, but being a positive fellow, Lurie himself characteristically thinks this an advantage, since he is free to consider contemporary events without the burdens of adolescent prejudices still hovering in his mind. In the years since 1967 he has become such an eager participant in the American scene, so compulsive a listener to car radio and watcher of television that the American parade, with its outsized performances, its flamboyance and sleaziness and occasional moments of glory, is as familiar to him as Golda Meir, Dayan, and Brezhnev. It is human nature he understands, and foreignness in no way disqualifies him from savoring the peculiarly American variety of the human comedy. Perhaps his late arrival, his status as an enthusiastically American alien, makes Lurie less acerbic in his partisanship than other cartoonists. But he himself doesn't feel his status inhibits him from seeing clearly and speaking freely.

Lurie already belongs among the elect in American cartooning. Like such talented men as Conrad, Oliphant, Wright, and D'Arcy, he came to the fore at a time when the field of political cartooning was more open than it was fifteen years ago, when in Europe and America Low, Vicky, Tim, Herblock, Mauldin, MacPherson, and Illingsworth were doing their best work. It is not necessary to denigrate others in the winner's circle to celebrate Lurie's merits. Lurie lacks Herblock's anger, scorn, and command of idiom, but not because he tries for scorn or anger and fails. His distinction lies elsewhere. You cannot tell from his cartoons, though you might make a shrewd guess, how Lurie would vote. Papers of many shades of political opinion take pleasure in publishing Lurie, but not because Lurie works at that familiar mediocre level of all-things-to-all-men that is the curse of many widely syndicated cartoonists who aren't sure what they think and are afraid to offend. Lurie is almost never vindictive or moralistic; what saves him from blandness is the sharpness of his judgment, conveyed by metaphor. His figures may be caught red-handed, may be overweening, stupid, or bereft of solutions. Lurie finds a comic equivalent of that predicament, and shows a *man* in that condition, and only incidentally is that man Nixon or McGovern or Mao. The exactness of the parallel that Lurie draws is the cream of the jest and the source of his bite.

I think Ranan Lurie is only beginning to get the recognition he deserves in the front rank of American cartoonists. This book shows how much he has already achieved.

THOMAS GRIFFITH

EDITOR

LIFE MAGAZINE

Thomas Griffith

LONG ISLAND, AUGUST, 1973

THE POLITICAL CARTOON AS THE ULTIMATE EDITORIAL

Some time ago I was interviewed by a group of psychiatrists and psychologists who, in preparing a book on the subject of creativity, contacted creators in such fields as the plastic arts, music, writing, and political cartooning. The first time I had talked to psychologists and psychiatrists on a professional basis (excluding a fifteen-minute interview by an air force psychiatrist who admitted me to fight pilot school when I was 16), I found it at the beginning a mesmerizing experience. However, it encouraged me to express feelings in words and parables.

I found myself saying that before starting my work on a cartoon, as I search for the political message, I feel like an astronaut who has just left Earth's gravity and is floating weightless in his capsule, not knowing where his floor, walls, and ceiling are. When I arrive at my desired message, it is not witty, not designed, not humorous, not sarcastic. It is a basic, crude, clumsy, but honest notion of what I want to say about a specific event. It is based on facts accumulated through much reading, consideration of background information, and knowledge about politicians, whom I try to meet personally so I may better anticipate political moves. Once I have found the message, I have found the floor of my capsule.

Once I have found the floor of my capsule, the ceiling and the walls are automatically established, standing in their natural relationship to the floor.

If the floor is the political message, the ceiling is the art, and the walls are the humor, the satire, the caricature, and the editorialization.

I then refine the crude, basic message—as crude oil is refined by machinery—through the mechanics of art, humor, sarcasm (if necessary), and timing. And as makeup may make a woman more attractive, so art, humor, and journalism may do the same for the basic message.

In brief, the political message is the crux of the cartoon. I once told a senior editor of *The New York Times* that to sense the real worth of a political cartoonist one must imagine that the cartoonist breaks his right hand and that his editor suggests to him that, since he cannot draw for the next three months, he should dictate a daily written editorial to his secretary. Having imagined this, one must answer the question, would that cartoonist, thus stripped of his graphic talent, be able to execute such a mission?

Since a political cartoonist is what his political message is, it must be his own. If he won't wear a suit that is not to his taste, he certainly won't "wear" a political interpretation that is not to his taste. I was amazed to find out when I came to this country that, historically, political cartooning is not independent here. Somehow, many American political cartoonists tend to be more editorial illustrators than political analysts. Every contract with a syndicate I have had includes a clear-cut definition of the absolute independence I should have from every point of view—analytically, graphically, and humorously—and I can't tell you how much havoc that created with every syndicate. My opinion was that this kind of professional freedom does not at all assure good political cartoons, but I can vouch for poor results from even an excellent cartoonist if he is not given this kind of independence.

The fact is that all the very best cartoonists in this country are politically independent, and get staunch support from newspapers who give them that carte blanche. Cartoonists like Herblock, Mauldin, and Oliphant are excellent because of their independence, among other reasons. (However, I don't want to confuse independence with an editor's or art director's good advice. This can be extremely beneficial to the analyst who, when the cartoon is being born, can use a "cold eye" that can see the facts he cannot. This advice should be based on the work already executed and of course the cartoonist may veto it.)

The only difference between a good editorial writer and a good political cartoonist is that the editorial writer does not know how to draw.

Thus, the good political cartoon is one editorial answer to television, for it fights the visual concept of the tube on equal grounds, and relates to young readers through a medium that they have been trained to look at for the last twenty years—the visual.

14

However, I must admit that all I have said until now can pop like a balloon filled with hot air if the so-called political cartoon is not good. The written editorial *can* tolerate average talent, while the editorial cartoon cannot. A good political cartoon and a poor political cartoon cannot be compared—it would be like a comparison between Candice Bergen and an attractive dummy in a Macy's window. While, basically, an editorial writer has to command two talents, political analysis and good writing a good political cartoonist should add three other talents, art, humor, and caricaturization; and therefore, we can still find many more potential political writers than potential political cartoonists. So what happens is that while we can choose among political writers and get the best of them, when we have to choose a political cartoonist, we find that those who effectively command the necessary five talents needed are extremely rare. Thus we settle for less and less, so that many times the only criterion for the publisher or the editor is, Can the guy draw?

What is even worse, this tendency establishes the entire profession of political cartooning—at least in this country—as a vassal profession that "by nature" is supposed to accept directions of thinking from the editor, who "by nature" is more knowledgeable and more trained in the field of political analysis than the illustrator, who can show his graphic talents only.

Every editor can quite precisely compute an evaluation of his cartoonist by simply distributing each one of the five qualities mentioned above according to the following proportions: about 40 percent for political analysis and about 15 percent for each of the other four talents.

The editorial cartoon is the most extreme expression of criticism that society will accept and tolerate. The cartoonist's weapon is the spearhead of the editorial page and should be given more leeway to be critical than any article. Although cartoonists through the centuries have been jailed by the rulers of their times—as, for instance, Daumier was when he drew King Louis Philippe in a manner that enflamed the touchy monarch—never in American history has a political cartoonist been successfully sued for his professional interpretations, whereas many writers have been.

The important point here is the more art you have in your work, the more independent you become, because the combination of a legitimate idea or subject with an art form creates a strong protected arena, so well defended that cartoonists almost always feel on the right side of the track, spiritually and pragmatically.

We are dealing here with the world's second most ancient profession. The very first editorial cartoonists were the prophets who lived four, three, and two thousand years ago. These men who were the spiritual leaders of their times, communicated their ideas to the masses by translating the political, military, and economic situations of the times into visual descriptions that made a lot of sense to the simple farmer and small merchant. (However, the prophets never used the element of humor in their messages. Humor was discovered by society thousands of years later.)

In Matthew 13, verse 34, it says: "Jesus spoke all these things to the people in parables: and without parables he did not speak to them."

Jesus, who was affected by the impact of parables and utilized them beautifully, instead of expanding on his concept of the Kingdom of Heaven says (in Matthew 13, verse 44): "it is a treasure hidden in the fields" . . . and you go and buy this field.

One can virtually see the editorial cartoon. And, in verse 47, Heaven is likened to the catch of a net which gathers fish of every kind—again, a graphic parable which would be readily understood by those of his followers who were fishermen. In exactly the same way, a good political cartoonist who lives in New Hampshire will use a parable of deep snow to emphasize a point, whereas a good editorial cartoonist who serves his readers in Florida will shy away from a parable about snow because his readers do not identify with it.

I believe that a sincere, dedicated political analyst and cartoonist must be nonpartisan. He is an instant historian, treating every event according to its own merit. It is impossible that one person, one state, one regime, will always be right or will always be wrong. Therefore, any political analyst or cartoonist who assumes that Nixon, for instance, can only do bad, can't be a professional analyst. The same goes for the cartoonist who thinks that Nixon can only do good. You cannot play tennis with the forehand only.

The moment of truth will come when the cartoonist gauges the margin of time from the day he drew the cartoon. Then he can see how clearly or unclearly he has evaluated the situation through his work. Eventually, the simple facts and reality always win. Then it becomes apparent that wishful thinking is meaningless and the capacity to evaluate and project and even predict the events that are happening will eventually cement the professional status and integrity of the cartoonist.

I believe that every person has the right to form his own opinion. However, the moment he wants to influence others, he should be extremely careful not to dedicate himself to an obvious pattern of thinking—not only for the sake of his credibility, but also to avoid being obvious and, therefore, boring. Cartoonists have very sophisticated booby traps to be aware of. If he is wishy-washy or does not cultivate political know-how and do his homework, a cartoonist can easily become a mere illustrator. The trouble is that there is no sound barrier to break between the two professions. One just skids into the status of illustrator without even realizing it. Being an illustrator is not all bad, of course, but it is important that you identify such a fact and not expect to be recognized as a political analyst if you are not one. An illustrator differs from a political cartoonist the way a singer differs from a poet.

A cartoonist—like an actor—needs a stage and a respectful producer-director so that he can flourish. The stage of course is the newspaper; the producer-director, the publishing-editor. I know of quite a few good talents who were humbled or even choked while making the publisher or the editor satisfied. For instance, a situation in which the cartoonist's talent is channeled to settle small skirmishes in his home town or to serve the particular sense of humor of a specific editor would make that cartoon obsolete for broader markets or syndication. When we speak about "freedom of the press" we should realize that this slogan applies to us, members of the press, as well. After all, a dominant publisher who wishes to make every inch of his newspaper comply with his personal way of thinking may be a calculated risk for any flourishing talent. The ideal editor, from the political cartoonist's point of view, would be the editor who, first of all, identifies the five different talents that are potential cartoonist's tools and then encourages that cartoonist as much as possible by giving him the space, exposure, and backing, together with the good "cold eye" of a sophisticated objective reader. An *editor who knows what to look for* will eventually develop for himself and his newspaper a powerful weapon.

During the period Thomas Nast's dramatic analysis of Tammany Hall appeared in *Harper's (The Art and Politics of Thomas Nast* by Morton Keller, page 181), "*Harper's* circulation tripled . . . ; bribes of hundreds of thousands of dollars were offered—as were threats such as cancellation of the city's order of Harper Brothers' textbooks. E. L. Godkin's *Nation* declared: 'Mr. Nast has carried political illustrations during the last six months to a pitch of excellence never before attained in this country, and has secured for them an influence on opinion such as they never came near having in any country.' Less graciously, but no less genuinely, Tweed observed: 'I don't care a straw for your newspaper articles, my constituents don't know how to read, but they can't help seeing them damned pictures.' "

RANAN R. LURIE

(Excerpted from a lecture given at the Sydney, Australia, Press Club)

SCANDALS

by Ranan Lurie

LURIE'S OPINION

© 1973 The New York Times, SPECIAL FEATURES Syndicate LURIE

"IS THAT YOU, SPIRO?"

by Ranan Lurie

"I'M ONE THOUSAND PERCENT BEHIND YOU"

U.S. Press

"AND AFTER WE SURRENDER—ONLY NAME, RANK, AND SERIAL NUMBER!"

"CAREFUL, EDGAR—THE LOAD IS TREMENDOUS!"

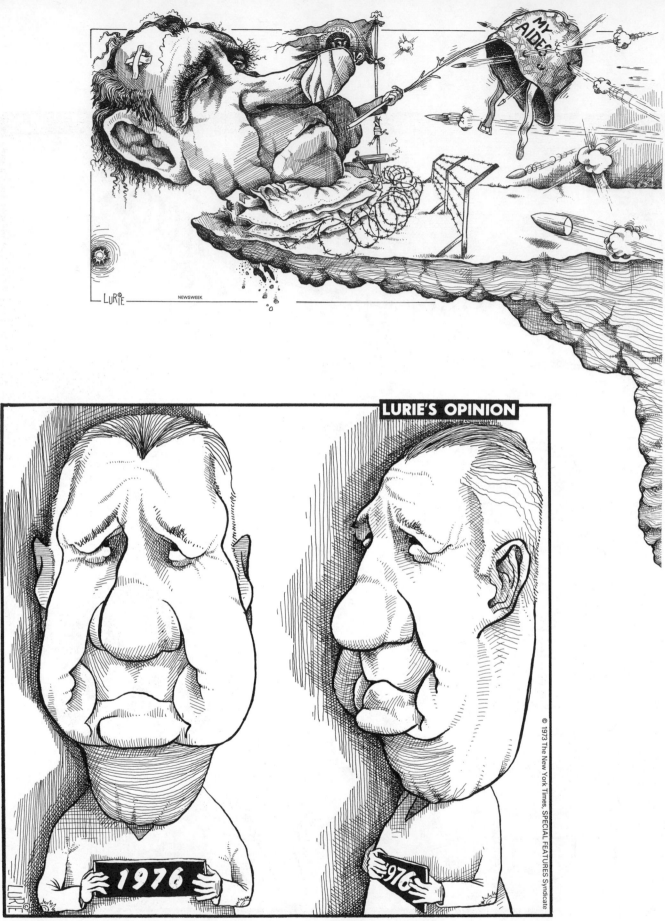

LURIE'S OPINION

1976

1976

© 1973 The New York Times, SPECIAL FEATURES Syndicate

8-22-73

ITT

LURIE

3-8-72

WATERGATE AFFAIR

LURIE

9-13-72

"PROUD TO BE YOUR FALL GUY, SIR!"

28

JUDGE JOHN J. SIRICA

MAYOR RIZZO OF PHILADELPHIA

SEN. EDWARD J. GURNEY (R-FLA.)

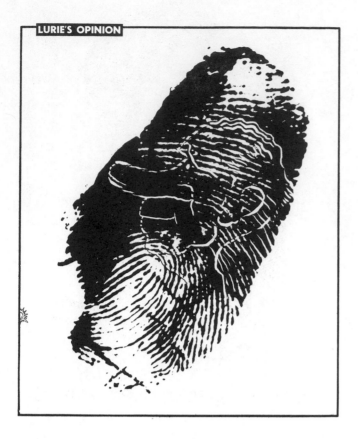

GRAY'S FINGERPRINT

IGNORANCE

COMPLICITY

WATERGATE

4-27-73

TOUGH POLITICAL CHOICE

33

4-12-73

34

"THE KING IS NAKED! THE KING IS NAKED!"

4-19-73

8-12-73

© 1973 The New York Times, SPECIAL FEATURES Syndicate

SS "EXECUTIVE PRIVILEGE"

"WELCOME ABOARD!"

WATER

GATE

LURIE

4-2-73

CLOSER AND CLOSER

LURIE'S OPINION

"WHAT CAN I DO FOR YOU, MR. TANAKA?"

MR. POLITICIAN

PENTAGON PAPERS

by Ranan Lurie

5-8-73

39

LURIE'S OPINION

PUBLIC OPINION

PROMISES

MY STAFF

INTERNATIONAL ACHIEVEMENTS

LURIE

5-15-73

40

5-25-73

"WELL—SO FAR I'M NOT HURT"

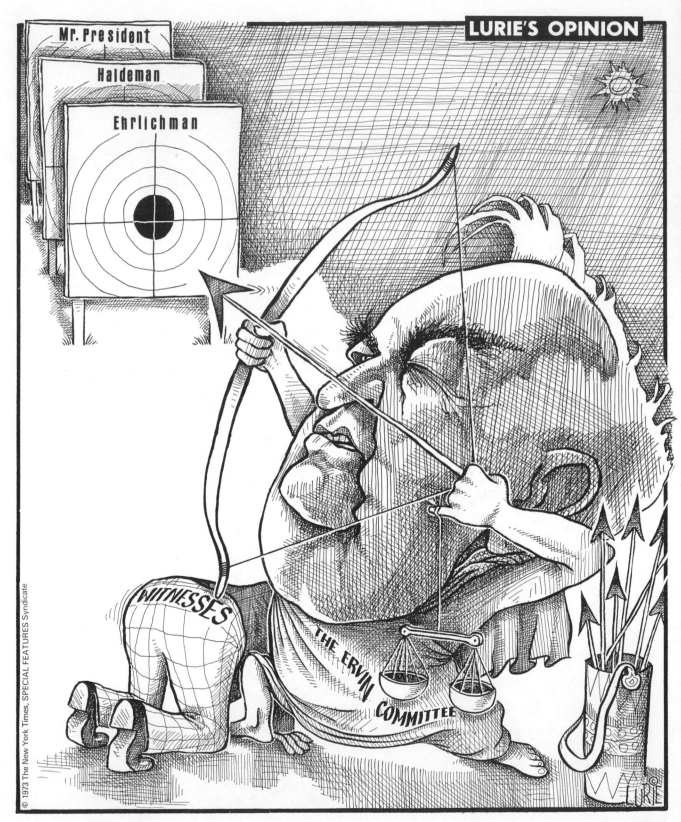

Mr. President

Haldeman

Ehrlichman

WITNESSES

THE ERVIN COMMITTEE

5-24-73

42

LURIE'S OPINION

Watergate

LuRiE

6-6-73

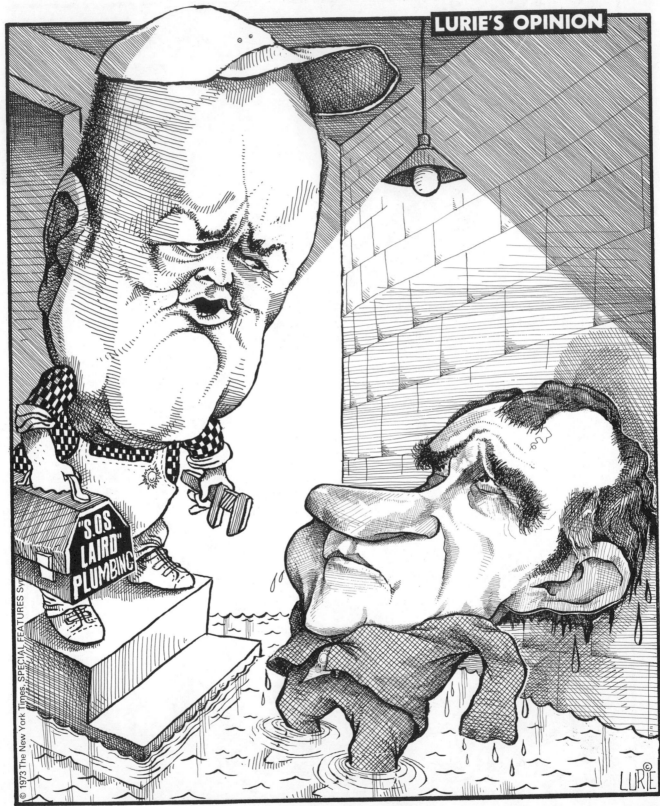

"S.O.S. LAIRD PLUMBING"

6-8-73

"SOME PLUMBERS YOU HAD HERE!"

44

ENERGY CRISIS

46

6-21-73

"ALL YOURS!"

BREZHNEVS VISIT

CONGR... WATERGATE ECONO...

"REMEMBER—ON MONDAY IT TURNS INTO A PUMPKIN!"

6-22-73

6-24-73

FALL FASHIONS

KICKBACK

"I AM A NOBODY. NO FILE ABOUT ME IN THE CIA, FBI, ETC."

6-27-73

PERSONALITIES

8-10-73

SPIRO

52   MAURICE STANS   DANIEL ELLSBERG

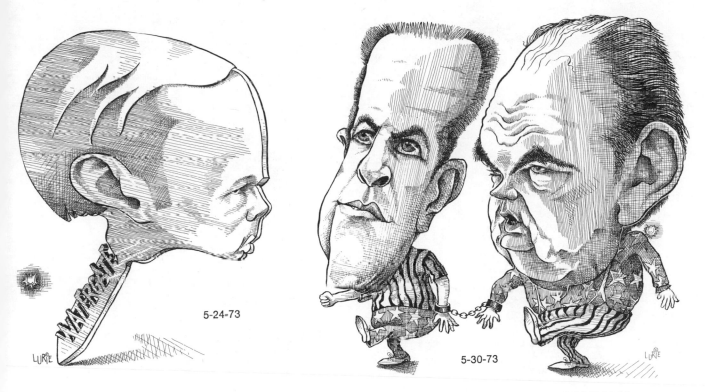

5-24-73

5-30-73

JOHN DEAN

HALDEMAN & EHRLICHMAN

MARTHA MITCHELL

JOHN MITCHELL

53

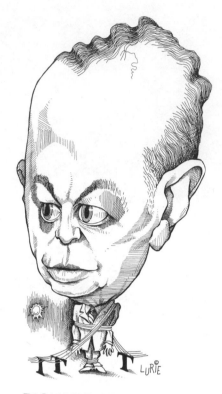

RICHARD KLEINDIENST

GRAY

6-14-73

SPECIAL WATERGATE PROSECUTOR
ARCHIBALD COX

PRESIDENT NIXON'S PERSONAL FRIEND
BEBE REBOZO

THE PRESIDENCY

INTEGRATION

LURIE'S OPINION

'72

NIXON'S POPULARITY POLLS

'73

© 1973 The New York Times, SPECIAL FEATURES Syndicate

LURIE

"M-M-MY FE-FELL-O-OW AME-ME-ME-RICANS!"

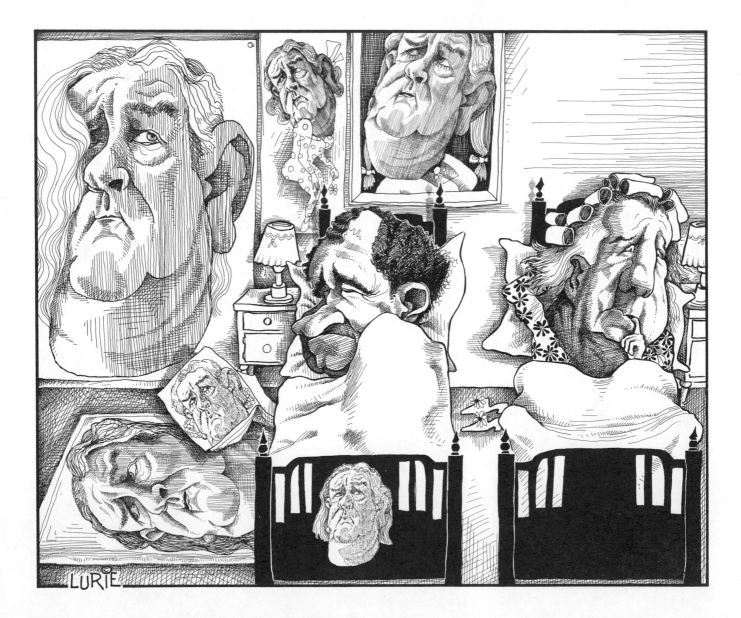

58

"COULDN'T YOU FIND BIGGER ONES?"

LURIE

4-15-71

LURIE©

1-14-72

"ATTENTION ALL COACHES..."

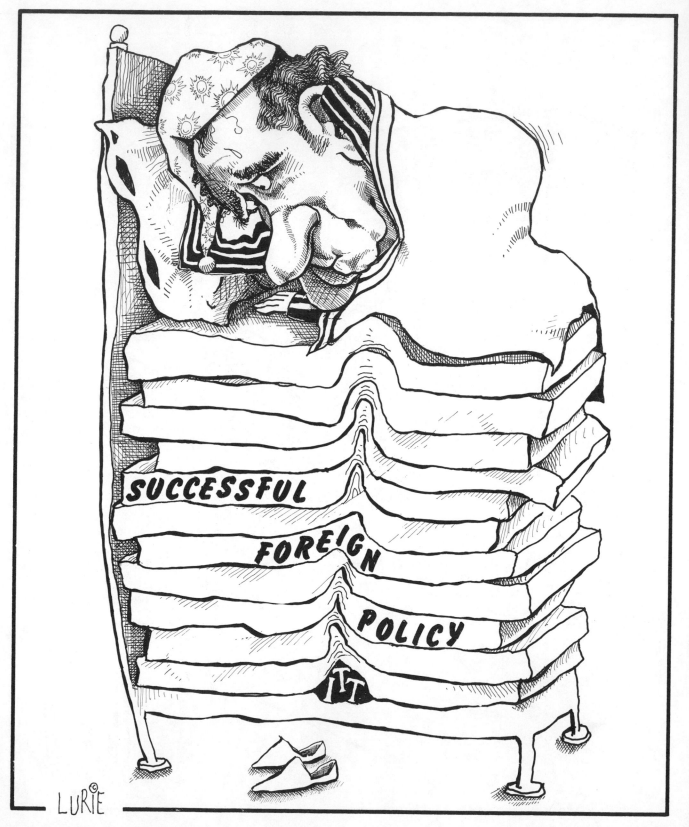

SUCCESSFUL FOREIGN POLICY

ITT

LURIE

3-31-72

LURIE'S OPINION

Speech

© 1973 The New York Times, SPECIAL FEATURES Syndicate

LURIE

THE PRESIDENT FIGHTS BACK

Life

4-15-72

"OK—WHO IS THE FBI INFORMER?!"

PRESIDENTIAL ELECTIONS

LURIE

5-22-72

THE RED CARPET

Life

6-8-72

11-9-72

66

"OK GUYS—LET'S SEE WHO FITS IN"

12-21-72

"AND NOW, A WORD FROM OUR SPONSOR"

MP DAVID

WHITE-
HOUSE

LURIE

12-4-72

5-9-73

"HOW DARE THEY BOMB THE INNOCENT?!"

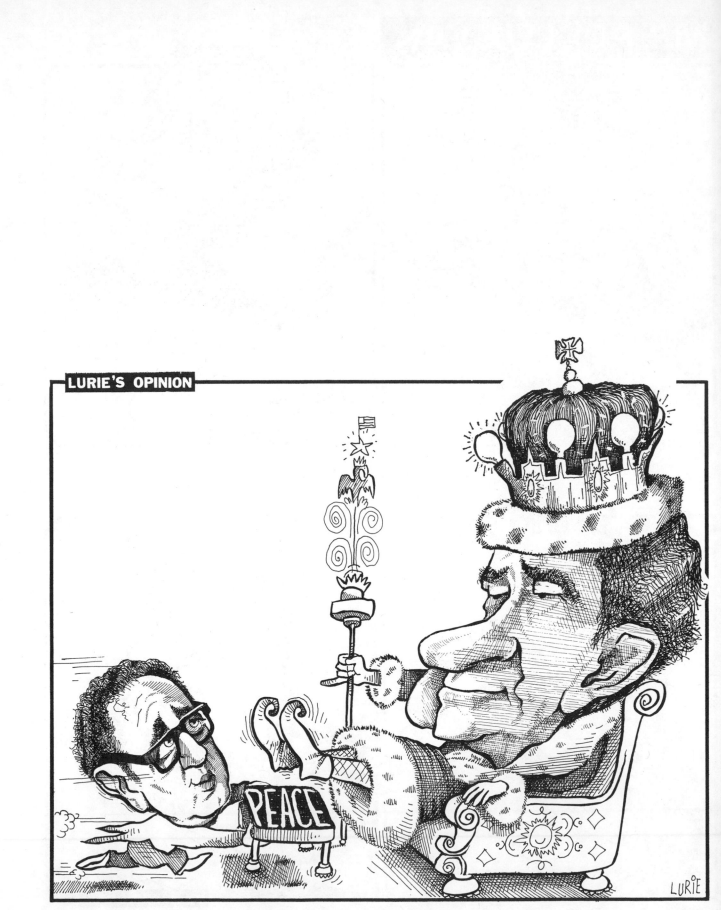

PEACE

LURIE

1-16-73

CONGRESS OPENS

1-3-73

RANAN LURIE IN NEWSWEEK

2-73, 5-73

MR. POLITICIAN

© 1973 The New York Times, SPECIAL FEATURES Syndicate

"CONGRATULATIONS - YOU MAY REPLACE ME!"

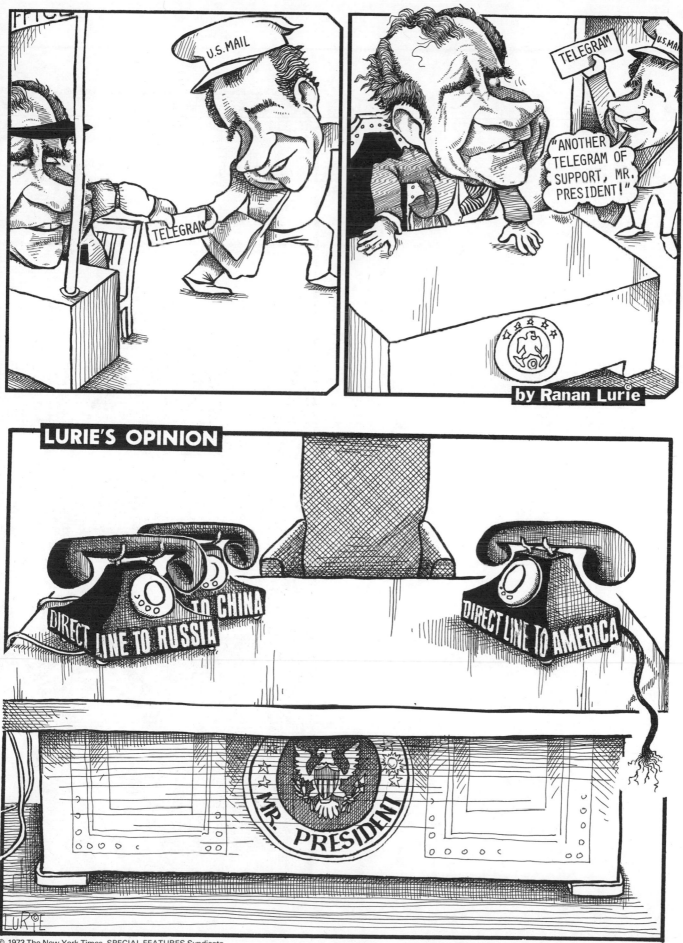

by Ranan Lurie

LURIE'S OPINION

9-18-73

© 1973 The New York Times, SPECIAL FEATURES Syndicate

"BECAUSE N O W IT'S THERE"

5-16-73

'I DO'

MR. POLITICIA

EXECUTIVE PRIVILEGE

LURIE

6-26-73

"THE LATEST 'ENEMY LIST,' SIR"

PERSONALITIES

Life

LBJ

SPIRO AGNEW

PAT NIXON

HENRY KISSINGER

GEN. ALEXANDER HAIG   RAMSEY CLARK   JOHN MITCHELL

MELVIN LAIRD

ELLIOTT RICHARDSON

WILLIAM P. ROGERS

CHIEF OF NAVAL OPERATIONS
ADMIRAL ELMO ZUMWALT

ROY L. ASH

DAVID K. E. BRUCE

JAMES R. SCHLESINGER

GEORGE BUSH

SCALI, OUR MAN IN THE UN

RICHARD HELMS, EX-CIA CHIEF

J. EDGAR HOOVER

EUGENE McCARTHY

REP. PETE McCLOSKEY

SEN. HENRY JACKSON

SEN. BIRCH BAYH

SEN. JOHN STENNIS

HUGH SCOTT

SEN. MIKE MANSFIELD

WILLIAM PROXMIRE

WILBUR MILLS

LESTER MADDOX

EX-MAYOR SAM YORTY

MAYOR RICHARD DALEY

GOV. NELSON ROCKEFELLER

GOV. NELSON ROCKEFELLER

JAMES BUCKLEY

BOBBY FISCHER

© 1973 The New York Times, SPECIAL FEATURES Syndicate

WILLIAM COLBY, CIA DIRECTOR

VIETNAM

LURIE

8-11-73

71

SOUTH VIETNAM'S BALLOT

DEMOCRACY

LURIE

9-27-71

LURIE

AIR FORCE

VIETNAM WAR

11-8-71

VIETNAMIZATION

LURIE

5-31-72

"NO, THERE WERE NO SECRET DEALS."

8-18-72

"LET'S STOP HORSING AROUND, DICK."

10-30-72

5-18-73

MR. POLITICIAN

PEACE

by Ranan Lurie

10-10-72

105

POLITICIAN'S BEST FRIEND

10-11-72

10-13-72

PEACE

LURIE

11-2-72

109

8-10-73

RUNNING OUT OF CANDLES

BOMBINGS

peace talks

12-22-72

"CA-A-AN'T H-E-AR Y-O-O-O-U!"

LURIE

12-20-72

MISSING IN ACTION

P.O.W.s

2-8-73

REBORN

2-5-73

THE WHEELER-DEALER

2-1-73

"OK, START FILLING!"

116

SOUTH-EAST ASIA

LURIE

4-23-73

5-17-73

118

8-2-73

119

LURIE©

5-31-73

"YOO HOO PAT - HAD A GOOD DAY IN OFFICE -
LOST ONLY CAMBODIA!"

PEACE AT LAST

PERSONALITIES

LE DUC THO

**SO. VIETNAM'S FORMER VICE PRES.
NGUYEN CAO KY**

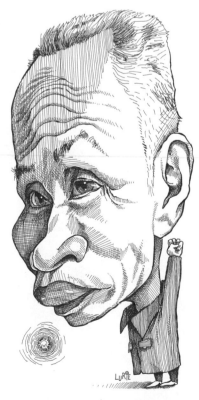

PHAM VAN DONG

GENERAL JOHN D. LAVELLE

GEN. CREIGHTON ABRAMS

NO. VIET DEFENSE MIN. GEN. VO NGUYEN GIAP

THE ECONOMY

THE TEXTILE PROBLEM

"NOW THAT YOU'VE LEARNED TO SIT, LET'S CONTINUE..."

TAX PAYER

LURIE
NEW YORK TIMES

1-71

129

LURIE

LURIE

7-27-71

270 DAYS

180 DAYS

90 DAYS FREEZE

LURIE

8-18-71

"LET'S SEE HOW WELL IT FLOATS"

8-16-71

"FREEZE!"

U.S. DOLLAR

LURIE

8-17-71

LURIE

8-5-71

10-7-71

"YOU'RE FREE—BUT BETTER WATCH OUT!"

10-29-71

BLOCKING THE VIEW

LURIE

11-16-71

"LET ME INTRODUCE THE NEW DOLLAR"

12-16-71

LURIE'S OPINION

"THEY MAY HAVE A POINT THERE, DOROTHY."

6-29-72

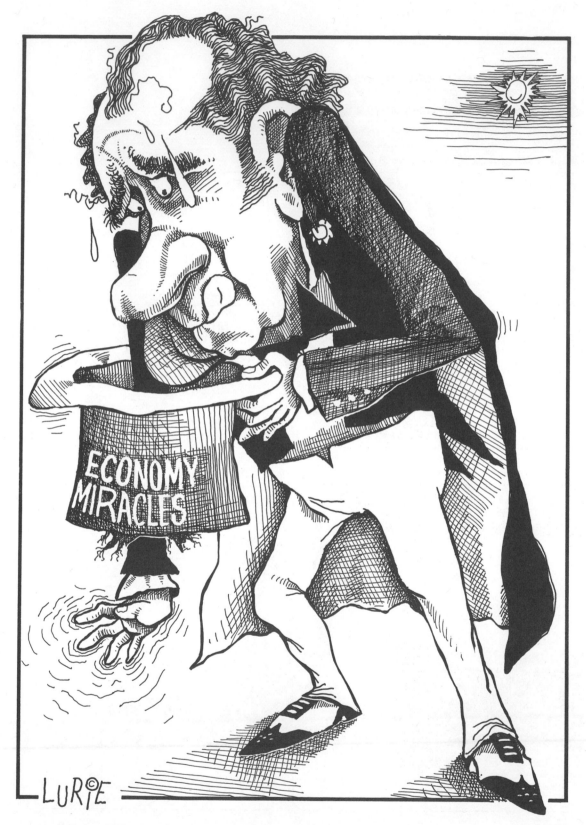

ECONOMY MIRACLES

LURIE

12-13-71

10-6-72

"I COMMAND YOU NOT TO RISE!"

FURTHER MOON PROJECTS

$

12-4-72

144

ECLIPSE

stock market

LURIE

2-14-73

145

LURIE'S OPINION

CANADIAN RAIL STRIKE

ECONOMY

LURIE

4-5-73

5-14-73

5-18-73

6-15-73

6-14-73

PERSONALITIES

GEORGE SHULTZ

6-21-73

JOHN CONNALLY

EARL BUTZ

CLAUDE S. BRINEGAR

THE COMMUNIST WORLD

DRAMA

PATHOS

CRY

HANDS

MOUTH

SINCERETY

by Ranan Lurie

U.S.S.R.

JAIL

LURIE

71

"OUR MACHINE ON THE MOON HAS ASKED THEM FOR POLITICAL ASYLUM"

CHINA

FOR-MOSA

DEM

LURIE

7-16-71

10-13-71

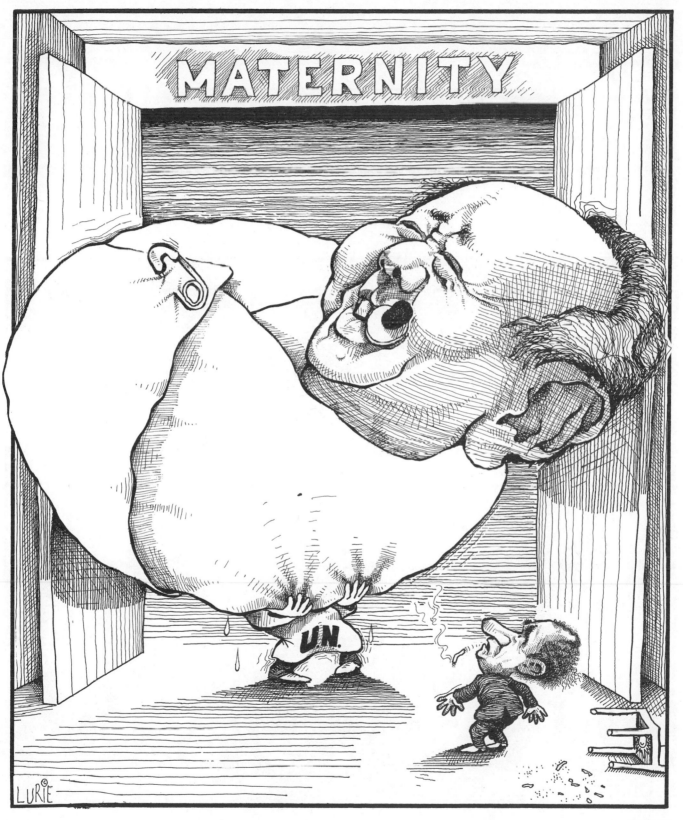

MATERNITY

LURIE

10-26-71

LURIE

HAVANA

10-21-71

10-27-71

10-6-71

166

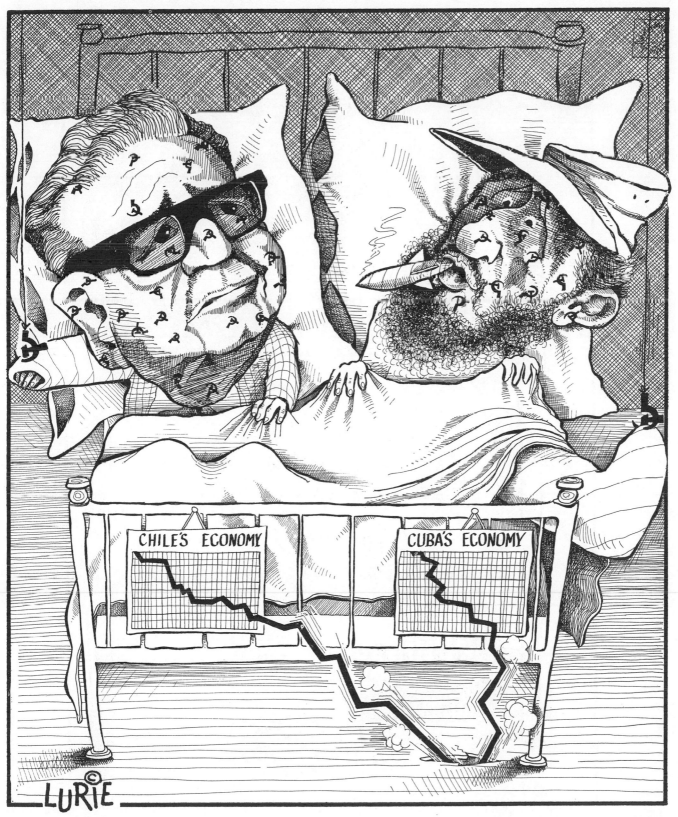

LURIE

11-9-71

INDIA'S
LEADERSHIP

COMMUNIST PARTY'S
SUPPORT

MRS. GANDHI

LURIE

12-5-71

LURIE

12-7-71

169

"BECAUSE IT'S THERE"

LURIE

12-7-71

LURIE

1-13-72

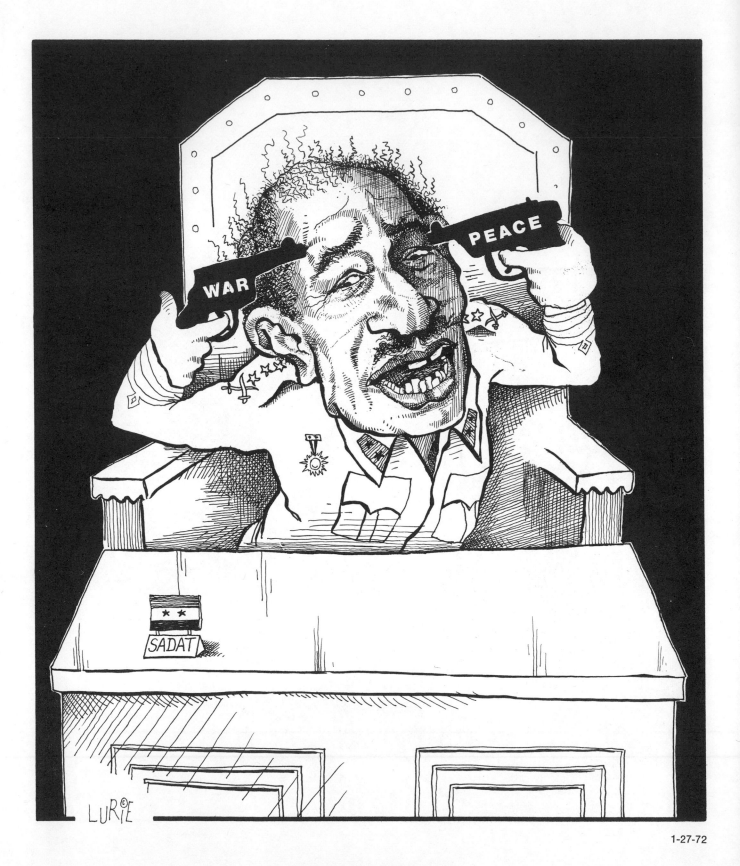

LURIE

1-27-72

RUSSIAN ROULETTE

ARMS PACT

6-13-72

ARMS PACT

7-19-72

"YOU'RE FIRED!"

LURIE

7-10-72

A MUZZLE

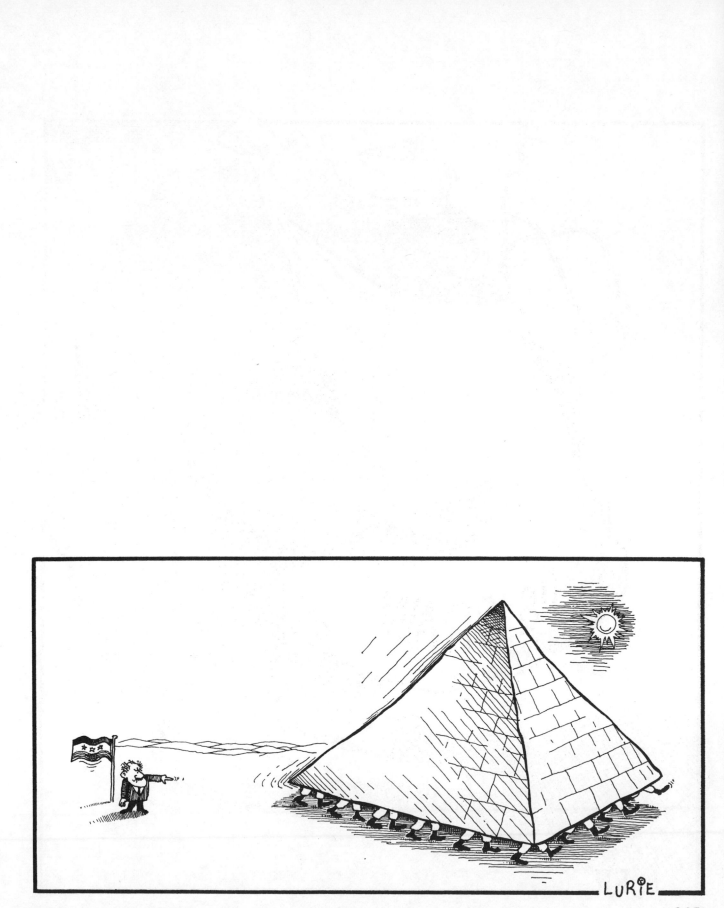

"THE RUSSIANS ARE GOING, THE RUSSIANS ARE GOING..."

8-2-72

12-7-72

"SO *YOU'RE* MY NEXT-DOOR NEIGHBOR"

INDO — CHINA

LURIE

2-5-73

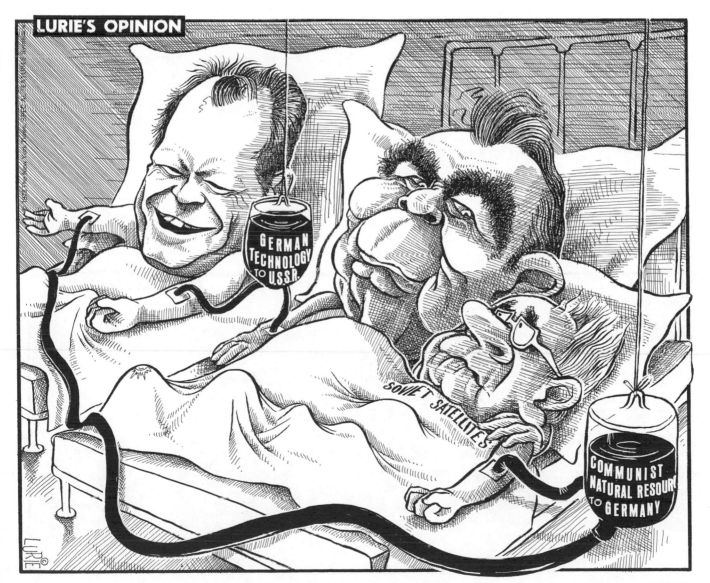

Der Spiegel

6-16-73

© 1973 The New York Times, SPECIAL FEATURES Syndicate

LURIE

6-10-73

U.S.S.R. CAVALRY TO THE RESCUE

9-11-73

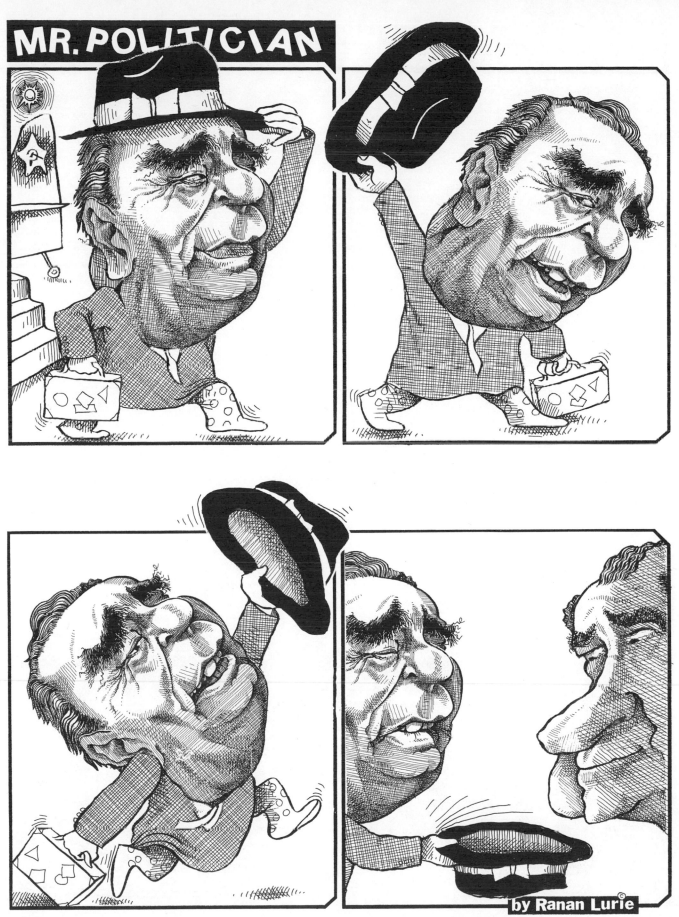

MR. POLITICIAN

by Ranan Lurie

6-20-73

6-19-73

6-20-73

PERSONALITIES

SALVADOR ALLENDE

JACOB MALIK

ANDREI GROMYKO

LEONID I. BREZHNEV

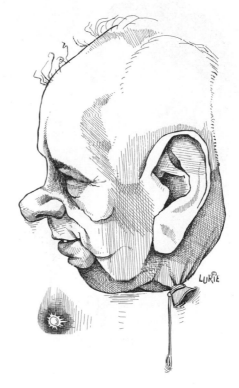

SOVIET PRESIDENT NIKOLAI PODGORNY

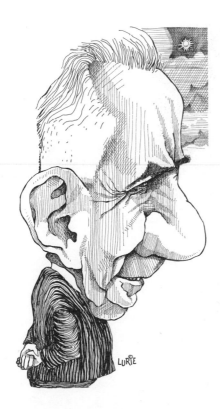

NIKOLAI KOSYGIN

187

CHUNG HEE PARK, S. KOREAN PRES.

GEN. HUANG CHEN.
CHINA'S MAN IN WASHINGTON

KUAN HUA, HEAD OF UN CHINESE DELEGATION

SOCIAL ISSUES

6-16-71

8-17-71

"BELIEVE ME, WALLACE—I *AM* DOING THE MINIMUM!"

193

LURIE

CITIES

MAYORS

8-6-71

9-16-71

LURIE

11-5-71

POLLUTION

LURIE

6-12-72

LURIE

DEFENSE BUDGET

Mc-GOVERN'S

NIXON'S

10-5-72

MY BUDGET

SOCIAL REFORM

1-31-73

"COME, COME—IT'S ONLY A MINOR CUT"

3-28-73

"THAT WILL TAKE CARE OF YOUR WOUNDED KNEE"

PERSONALITIES

GOV. GEORGE WALLACE

SHIRLEY CHISHOLM

GEORGE MEANY

CASPAR WEINBERGER

INTERNATIONAL

LURIE'S OPINION

PERON

6-23-73

HOMECOMING

"GOOD BOY—YOU ATE EVERYTHING!"

JAPAN

MADE IN RED CHINA

LURIE

8-24-71

8-23-71

"BROTHER—CAN YOU SPARE A MARK?"

EMPIRE

LURIE

NORTH IRELAND

9-9-71

209

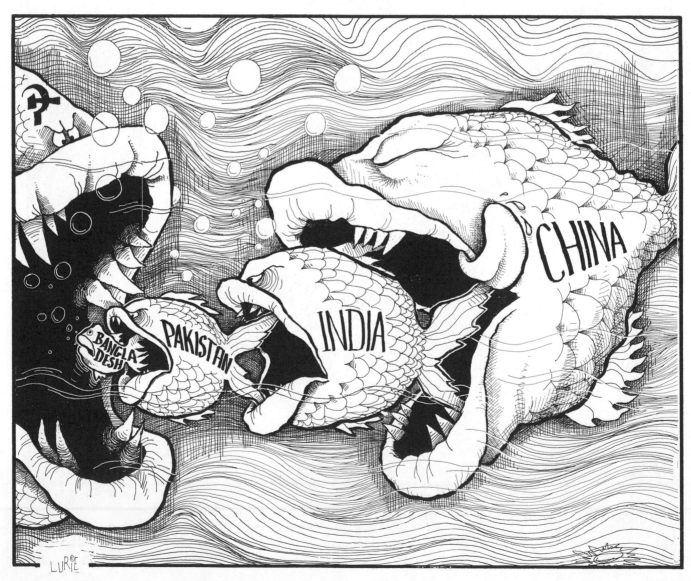

12-6-71

8-28-72

"YOU MAKE ME FEEL AT HOME"

LURIE'S OPINION

NO ENTRY
NO ENTRY
DEAD END
DEAD END
DEAD END
NO ENTRY
DEAD END
DEAD END
NO ENTRY
DEAD END
NO ENTRY
TRY
NO ENTRY

CHILE

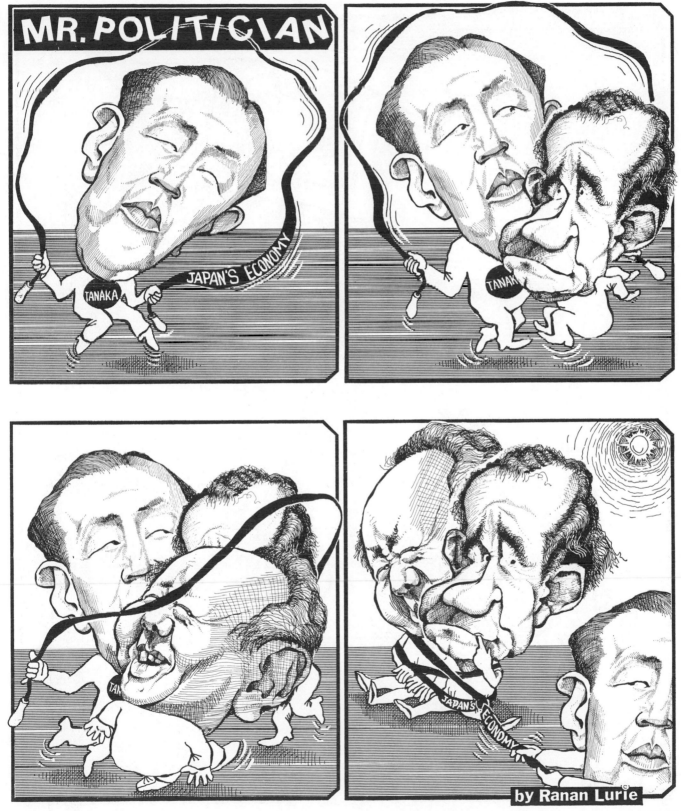

MR. POLITICIAN

TANAKA

JAPAN'S ECONOMY

by Ranan Lurie

8-29-72

6-12-73

"YOUR NEW LEADER"

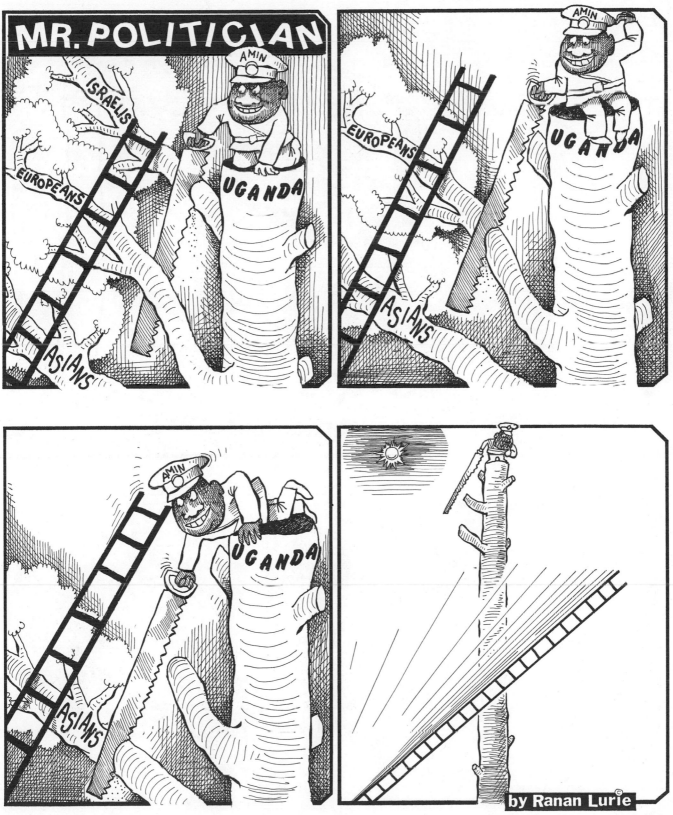

LURIE'S OPINION

2-15-73

4-25-73

"HI, UNCLE—WHAT DID YOU BRING ME THIS TIME?"

5-11-73

GOUGH WHITLAM, AUSTRALIA'S PREMIER

WEST GERMANY

EAST GERMANY

U.N.

LURIE

6-29-73

WATERGATE

ATLANTIC CHARTER

W. EUROPE

LURIE

5-17-73

6-1-73

"BRITANNIA RULES THE WAVES"

6-9-73

DISCOVERING THE YO-YO

6-4-73

8-22-73

ARGENTINA

Isabel Peron

LURIE

LURIE'S OPINION

CHILE

MARXISM

LURIE

'air!'

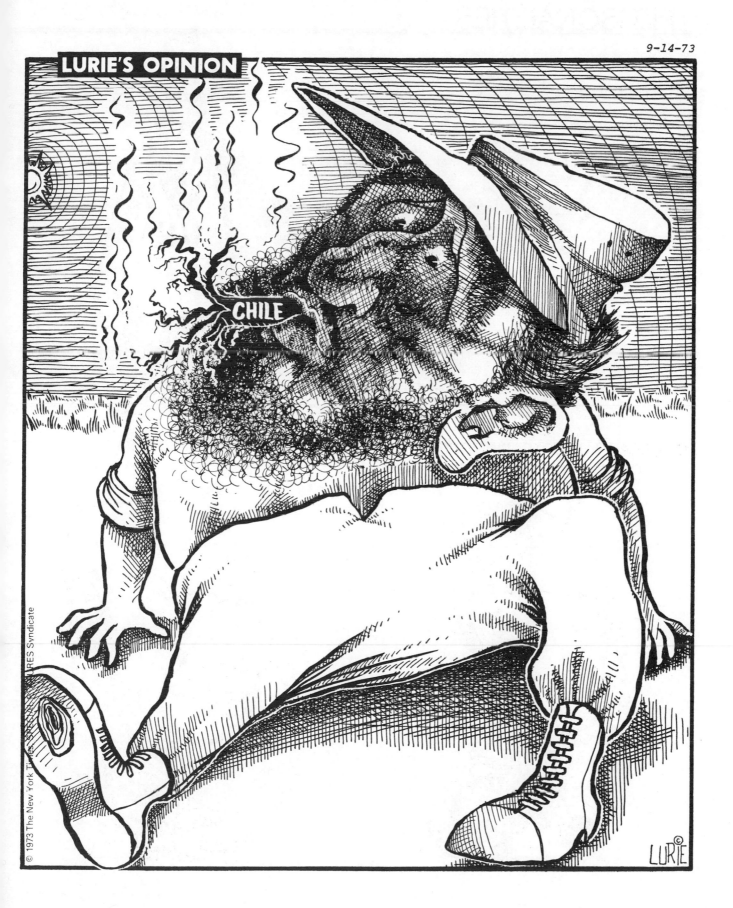

225

PERSONALITIES

GENERAL AUGUSTO PINOCHET UGARTE
COMMANDER OF CHILE'S ARMY

KURT WALDHEIM

U THANT

CHIANG KAI SHEK

226

EMPEROR HIROHITO

PRIME MINISTER
KAKUEI TANAKA

TAKEO FUKUDA

EISAKU SATO

MASAYOSHI OHIRA,
FOREIGN MINISTER

PHILIPPINE PRESIDENT,
FERDINAND MARCOS

PRINCE SOUVANNA PHOUMA

SHEIK MUJIBUR RAHMAN
OF BANGLADESH

PRES. BHUTTO OF PAKISTAN

228

PRES. HABIB BOURGUIBA OF TUNISIA

**ARCHBISHOP MAKARIOS,
PRES. OF CYPRUS**

HAILE SELASSIE

IDI AMIN OF UGANDA

229

DR. HECTOR J. CAMPORA
OF ARGENTINA

JUAN PERON

FIDEL CASTRO

BERNADETTE DEVLIN

ERSKINE CHILDERS,
PRES. OF IRISH REPUBLIC

GEORGES POMPIDOU

EDWARD HEATH

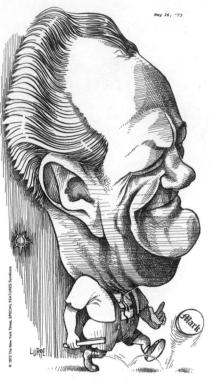

WILLY BRANDT

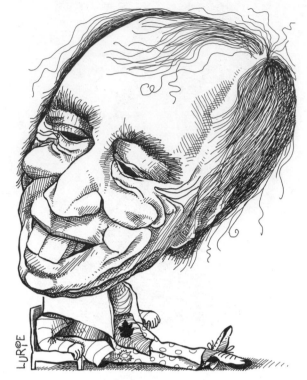

PIERRE TRUDEAU

MARSHALL TITO

PREMIER PAPADOPOULOS OF GREECE

THE MIDDLE EAST

8-7-73

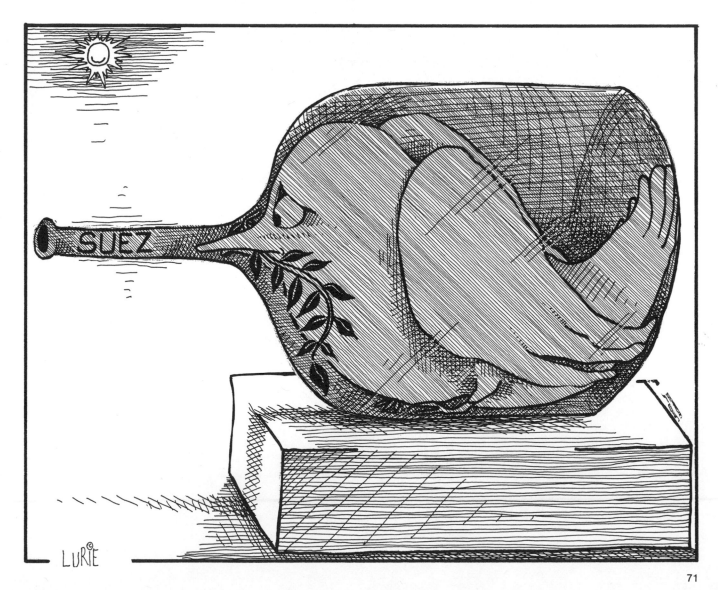

71

"ACCEPT MY TERMS—AND I'LL BE YOUR FRIEND FOR THE REST OF MY LIFE"

RANAN LURIE IN NEWSWEEK

9-3-71

"WE'RE MUCH STRONGER NOW"

LURIE

3-1-72

LURIE

6-13-72

LURIE'S OPINION

SADAT

KADAFI

LIBYA

EGYPT

JUST MARRIED

LURIE

8-3-72

241

8-9-72

242

TERRORISM

ARAB
GOVERNMENTS

LURIE

9-7-72

"AS LONG AS YOU KEEP ME OUT OF IT"

RETURN TO SENDER

VIOLENCE

LURIE

9-26-72

OIL

4-4-73

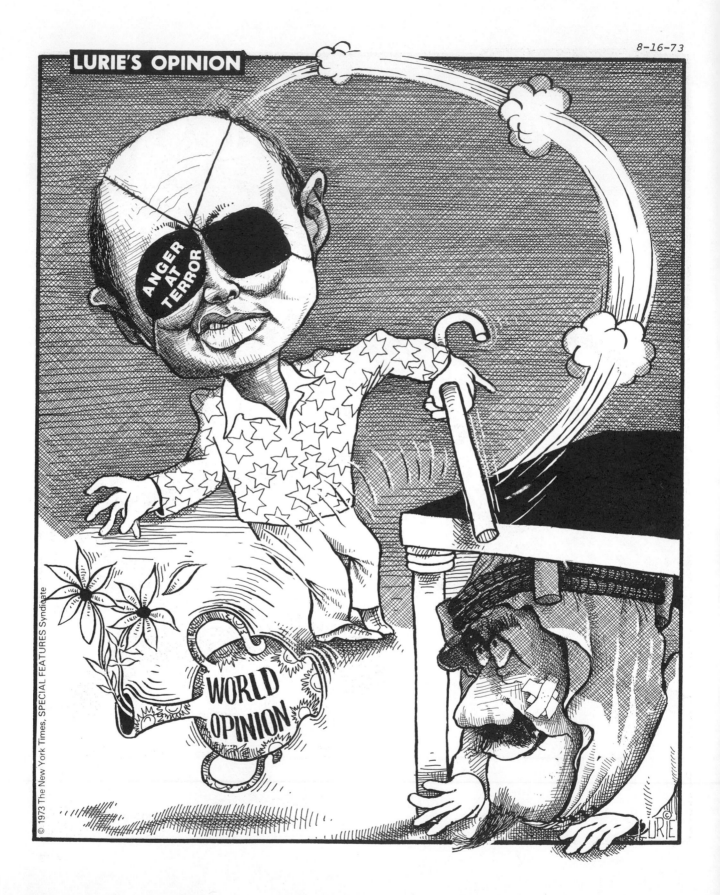

8-16-73

ANGER AT TERROR

WORLD OPINION

LURIE

246

MR POLITICIAN

by Ranan Lurie

3-13-73

LURIE'S OPINION

LEBANON

Syria

5-11-73

7-5-73

PERSONALITIES

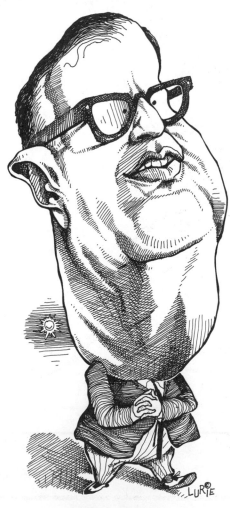

ABBA EBAN

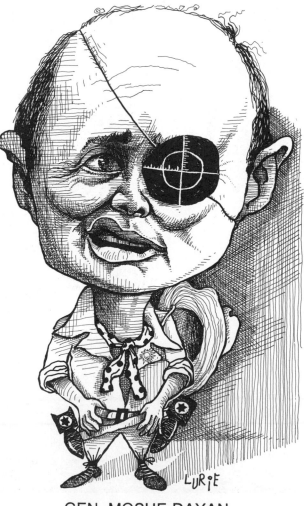

GEN. MOSHE DAYAN

YASSIR ARAFAT, AL FATAH CHIEF

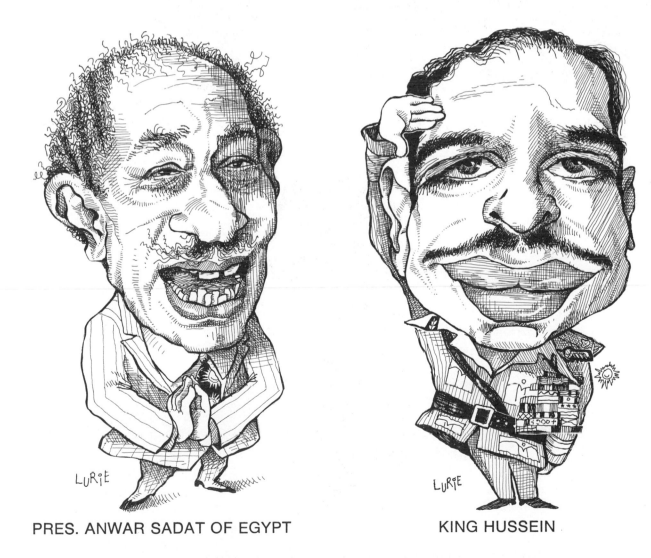

PRES. ANWAR SADAT OF EGYPT

KING HUSSEIN

KING HASSAN OF MOROCCO

COL. MUAAMER EL KADAFFI

KING FAISAL OF SAUDI ARABIA

CAMPAIGN '72

6-72

LURIE

ISSUES

255

6-72

"NOW, BE CAREFUL WITH YOUR ANSWER—AT THIS
MOMENT YOU REPRESENT ABOUT ONE MILLION PETS"

6-26-72

AMERICAN CONSERVATIVES

COMMUNIST WORLD

7-24-72

TEAM WORK

by Ranan Lurie

8-15-72

SHRIVER

LURIE

8-7-72

"NOW THAT YOU'RE HERE, LET'S GET THEM!"

LURIE

8-23-72

263

HITTING THE BULL'S EYE

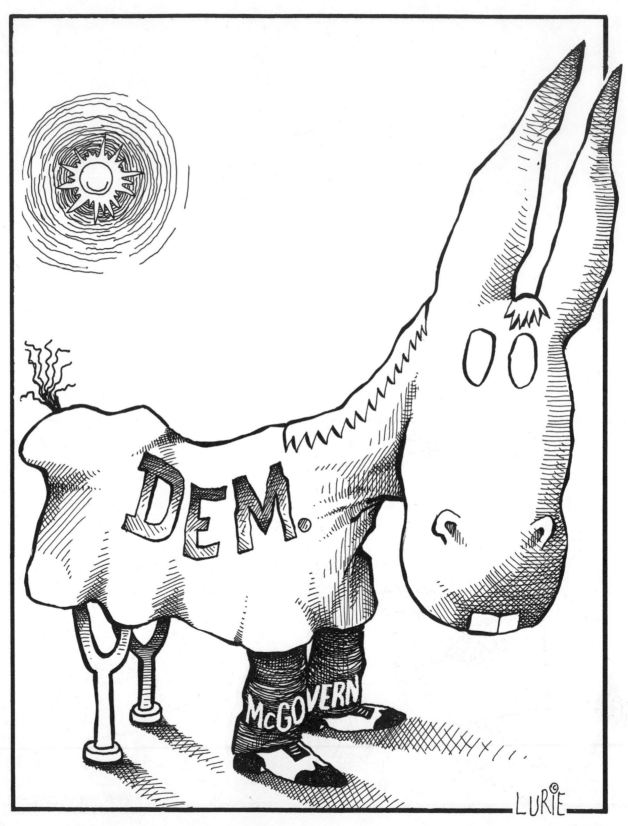

DEM.

McGOVERN

LURIE

8-11-72

266

LURIE

8-2-72

LOOKING FOR A RUNNING MATE

McGOVERN

NIXON

MEANY

LURIE

9-5-72

"I'M COMPLETELY NEUTRAL"

9-11-72

"OPERATOR—I WANT TO REPORT ANOTHER BUGGING INCIDENT"

FORMER IMAGE

LURIE

Time

10-2-72

THE REAL CAMPAIGN FIGHT

by Ranan Lurie

11-8-72

6-20-72

"IT'S OK—NO ONE'S LISTENING"

FOUR MORE YEARS

PERSONALITIES

GEORGE McGOVERN

EDMUND MUSKIE

HUBERT H. HUMPHREY

EDWARD KENNEDY

JOHN SCHMITZ, AM. PARTY NOMINEE

CLARK MacGREGOR

LARRY O'BRIEN

EX-CHAIRMAN WESTWOOD

LOWELL P. WEICKER

STOP THE PRESS

9-12-73

"WE'RE GOING TO MAKE YOU AN OFFER YOU CAN'T REFUSE"

"SINCE THE KIDS GET ALONG SO WELL, WE CAN GO ON MEETING"

281

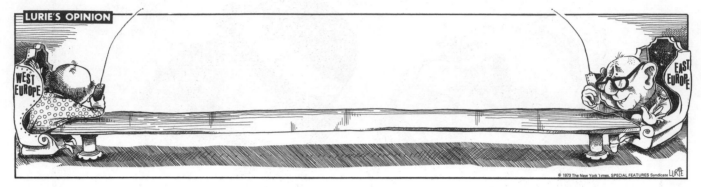

7-5-73

6-30-73

EXPLOSIVE DOMINOES

FOREIGN POLICY

WATERGATE

LURIE
NEWSWEEK

8-1-73

MR. POLITICIAN

MARXISM

LURIE'S OPINION

Australia's coming recognition of Cuba

GOUGH WHITLAM
AUSTRALIA'S PREMIER

7-31-73

"I SAY—CAN YOU GIVE ME A MATCH?"

9-19-73

by Ranan Lurie

LURIE'S OPINION

LURIE'S OPINION

© 1973 The New York Times, SPECIAL FEATURES Syndicate

WALDHEIM'S MID-EAST PEACE TRIP

LURIE

7-8-73

"NEW '74 AMERICAN MODELS JUST OUT"

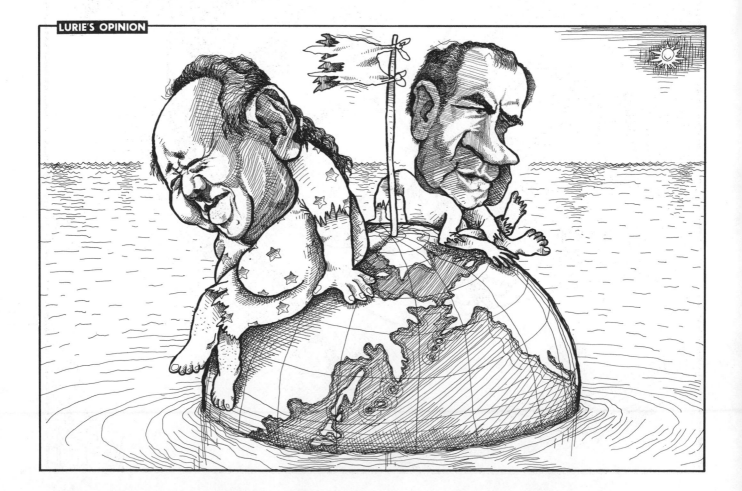

"SHE LOOKS BETTER AS THE YEARS GO BY"

7-6-73

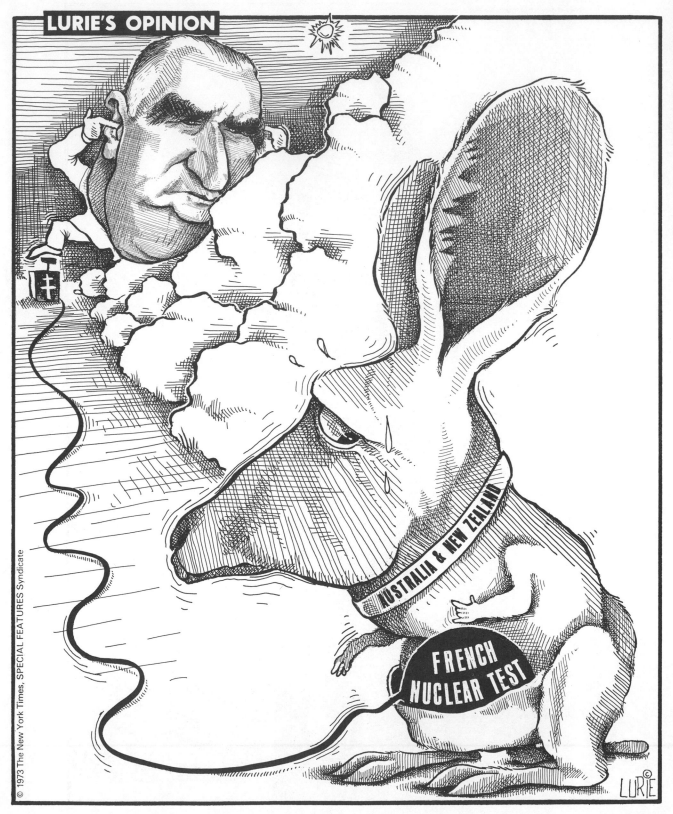

LURIE'S OPINION

AUSTRALIA & NEW ZEALAND

FRENCH NUCLEAR TEST

LURIE

7-21-73

LURIE'S OPINION

FRENCH NUCLEAR TESTS

WORLD OPINION

AUSTRALIA & NEW ZEALAND NAVIES

LURIE

DAVID AND GOLIATH

9-19-73

RETREATING INTO A LONG COLD WINTER

7-8-73

LURIE

LURIE'S OPINION

SADAT

KADDAFI

ARAB LEADERSHIP

7-29-73

"THIS PYRAMID AIN'T BIG ENOUGH FOR THE BOTH OF US"

LURIE'S OPINION

EGYPT

LYBIA

WAR

LURIE

7-10-73

"SIC 'EM, BOY!"

"CHANGE YOUR POLITICAL COURSE!"

7-21-73

"LIGHT AT THE END OF THE TUNNEL"

7-24-73

7-19-73

9-15-73

LURIE'S OPINION

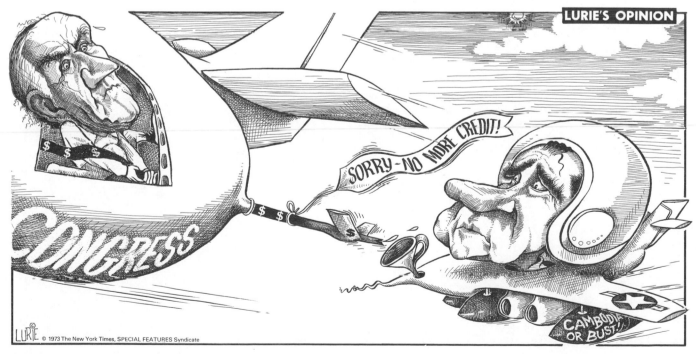

LURIE'S OPINION

7-18-73

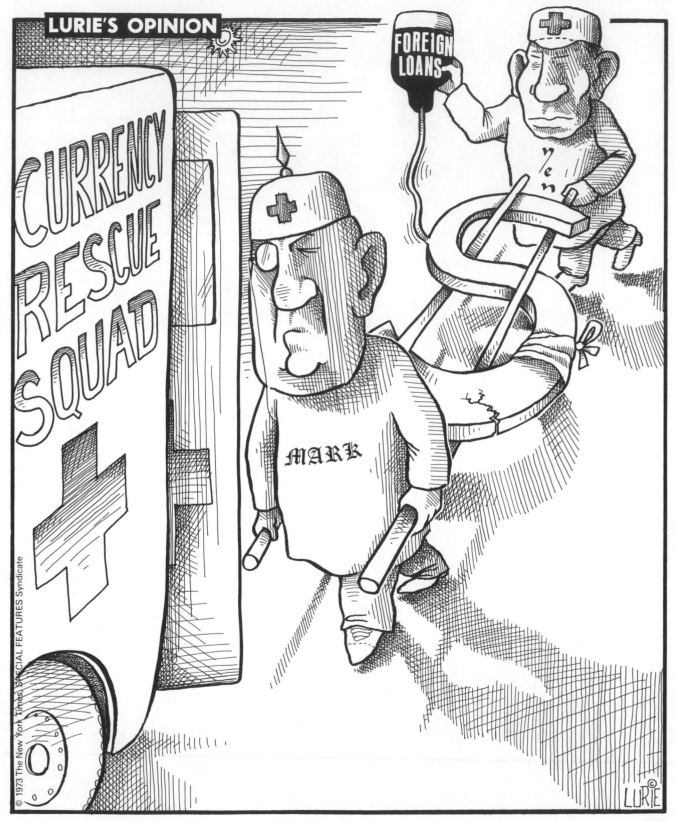

7-12-73

LURIE'S OPINION

7-27-73

"SAY IT WITH FLOUR"

7-12-73

7-6-73

303

9-5-73

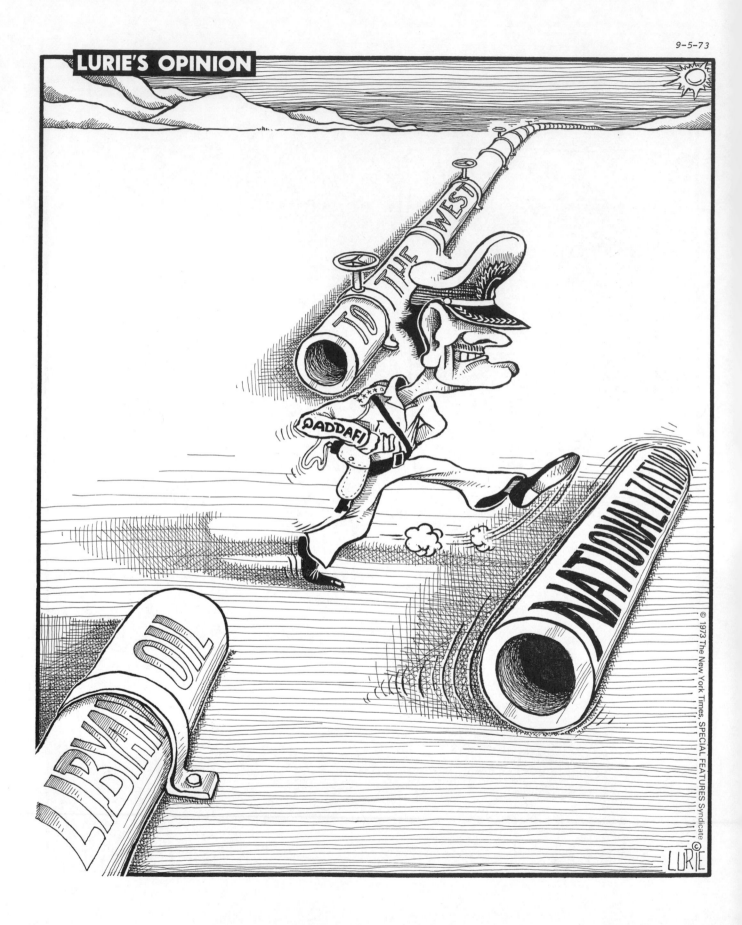

MR. POLITICIAN

by Ranan Lurie

7-18-73

305

WALLACE'S BUSING SYSTEM

7-18-73

THE SPIRIT OF '76

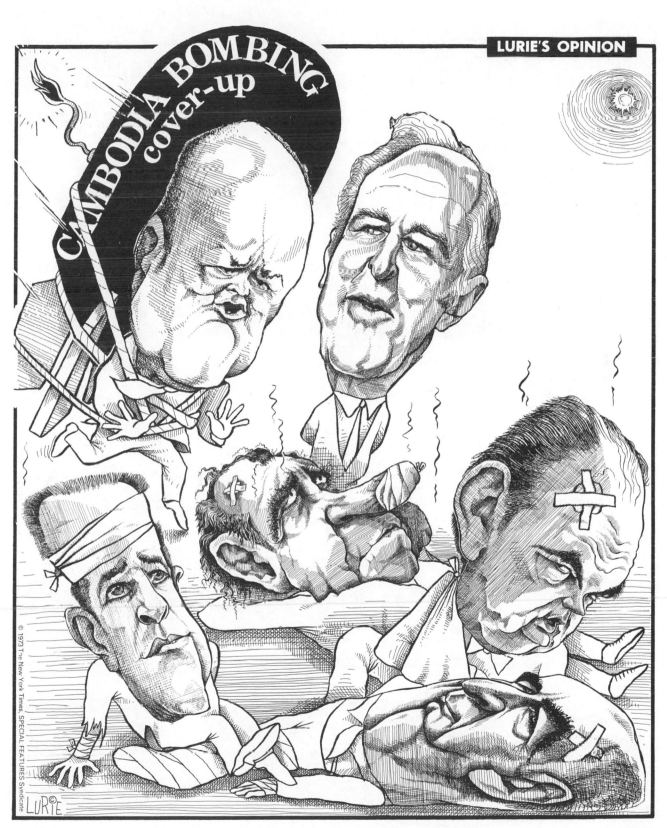

CAMBODIA BOMBING cover-up

7-26-73

"I GUESS THE WORSE IS OVER NOW, FELLOWS"

307

LURIE'S OPINION

WHITE HOUSE PAPERS

7-14-73

"THE PRESIDENT WILL BE GLAD TO SEE YOU, SENATOR ERVIN, AFTER LUNCH"

LURIE'S OPINION

7-11-73

"ABOUT WATERGATE: I WANT TO MAKE IT PERFECTLY UNCLEAR..."

7-15-73

310

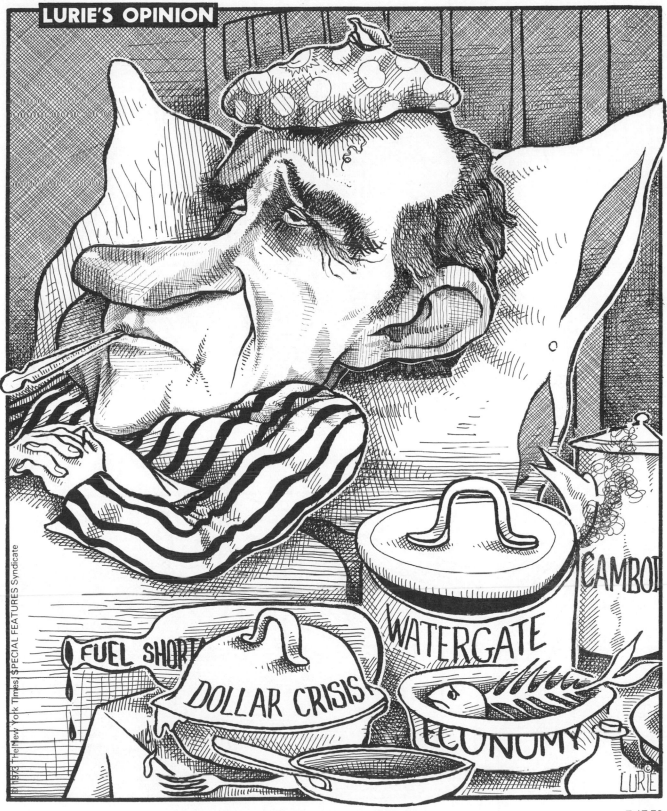

7-17-73

"I CAN'T BELIEVE I ATE THE WHOLE THING"

"GOOD MORNING, MR. PRESIDENT"

7-25-73

LURIE'S OPINION

Arab oil invest-ments

WESTERN ECONOMY

PERSONALITIES

SENATOR SAM J. ERVIN JR.

SENATOR HOWARD H. BAKER, JR.

7-24-73

SEN. LOWELL P. WEICKER

8-1-73

SENATOR ABE RIBICOFF

7-27-73

**DR. HERBERT STEIN,
CHAIRMAN OF COUNCIL OF
ECONOMIC ADVISERS**

7-21-72

**ARTHUR F. BURNS, FEDERAL
RESERVE BOARD CHAIRMAN**

316

7-14-73

EXILED PRINCE NORODOM SIHANOUK
OF CAMBODIA

7-8-73

PRESIDENT LON NOL OF CAMBODIA

6-30-73

PREMIER CHOU EN-LAI

317

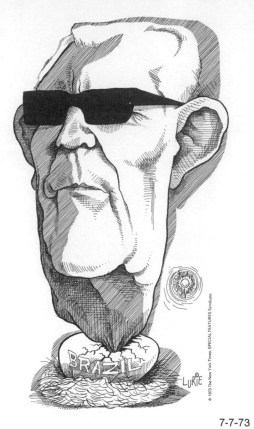

7-7-73

PRESIDENT-SELECT ERNESTO GEISEL

7-22-73

SHAH OF IRAN,
MOHAMMAD REZA PAHLAVI

6-30-73

NORMAN KIRK, PRIME MINISTER OF NEW ZEALAND

BIOGRAPHY

When the editors of *Life* magazine decided to engage its own political cartoonist, they flew Ranan Lurie each week from Montreal, where he was then exhibiting, in order to get one cartoon a week from the artist described in the *Sydney Sun Herald* as "the cream of political cartoonists . . . one of the world's leading political cartoonists . . . a master of his craft." In the two years that his cartoons have been available in nationwide syndication he has swept the prizes of the Montreal Salon of Cartoonists, the prestigious Headliners Award, a Front Page Award from the Newspaper Guild of New York, and has been nominated by his peers in the National Cartoonists Society of America, in a nation-wide secret ballot as one of the three Best Editorial Cartoonist of of 1971, and also of 1972.

Now an American resident, Lurie's daily and Sunday political cartoons are distributed nationally and internationally by The New York Times Special Features Syndicate, appearing in more than 140 newspapers, from the *Los Angeles Times* and the *Honolulu Advertiser* to the *Boston Globe* and the *Philadelphia Inquirer*; from the *Montreal Star* and the *Des Moines Register and Star* to the *Houston Post* and the Columbia (S.C.) *State Journal*; from *Newsweek* magazine and *Der Spiegel* to newspapers in Iran and Australia. His cartoons are seen and enjoyed by more than 20 million readers in the United States alone.

Born in 1932, a sixth-generation Israeli, Ranan Lurie studied art in Jerusalem and Paris, and was considered Israel's national cartoonist. With a background in the fine arts (he created the "expandable painting" which the Guggenheim Museum described as a "first in art"), Lurie manages to blend the tradition of fine arts and political analysis. A regular contributor to *Newsweek*—and the only editorial cartoonist to make the front pages of the *Wall Street Journal*—he is equally well known in this country through his oil paintings. Governor Nelson Rockefeller, then-Secretary of Defense Melvin Laird, Secretary of State William P. Rogers, Vice President Agnew, well-known actors, and leading personalities in all areas of society have sat for him for their portraits and caricatures.

He is a member and lecturer of the Fine Arts Department at the University of Haifa, which he visits annually for a series of lectures on Political Cartooning and Fine Arts.

The influence and prestige of his cartoons is such that party differences have been shelved to honor Lurie and his "victims" at an official reception in the Senate sponsored by Senators Abraham Ribicoff and Lowell Weicker, representing both major parties—the first time such an event has taken place in the Senate.

At twenty-two he won the highest award of the Federation of Journalists in Israel—not for his drawing but for his writing. He has held twenty-two exhibitions in America, Europe, and Israel, and his work appears regularly in the Sunday *London Times, Paris Match,* and the *International Herald Tribune.*

Lurie served as a reserve combat major with the Israeli Paratroopers, and trained with the U.S. 101 Airborne Division, the 16th Independent Brigade of the British Paratroopers, and with the Paratroopers of the French Foreign Legion.

He now lives in his country home in Greenwich, Connecticut, with his wife, Tamar, and their three children—Rod, Barry, and Daphni. His hobbies —tennis—and cartooning, of course.